heir of sisyphus

adrija ghosh is a polyglot poet, writer, & translator dedicated to decolonization and diversity in academia & the arts. Her debut poetry pamphlet, *the commerce between tongues*, was published by Broken Sleep Books in 2023. Her works explore the complexities of language & the polycultural body, and can be found in *Gutter Magazine, bath magg, Wasafiri,* & *Modern Poetry in Translation* amongst others. Currently, she is translating the autofiction of her favourite poet, Jibanananda Das. Find her via @byadrija.

Also by adrija ghosh

the commerce between tongues (Broken Sleep Books, 2023)

CONTENTS

ISBN: 978-1-916938-35-9

Cover designed by Aaron Kent

Edited and Typeset by Aaron Kent

Broken Sleep Books Ltd
PO BOX 102
Llandysul
SA44 9BG

heir of sisyphus

adrija ghosh

Broken Sleep Books

the human hippocampus is responsible for our memory, dreams, and imagination. i think we took our temporal lobe and called it love. we made a house in there. the bricolage came and stuffed it with birdsong. i filled it with thunderstorms. my fists full with childhood. the house of my brain, a vineyard of windchimes. the hippocampus drunk on the very first firsts.

memory, dreams, imagination are interchangeable.
dreams are an interlude. they are parentheses. an afterthought in articulation.

an octopus changes colour while it dreams in its sleep, turning canary from ivory, pulsating like a lighthouse underwater. and i wonder: if the best of us show our true colours when we spell out our dreams too.

the etymology of 'dream' roots it in *deception*, meaning: the very nature of a dream is to be false. in my dreams, thus, even you can't live up to the idea of you. call it imagination. **the realm of the hippocampus.**

i dream of you – is this ambition?

if ambition is desire, then wanting you is an enterprise. a full time job. a labour of hubris.

(ambition is arrogance. but so is love.)

i want you. is desire greed?

i want to tell myself i am better than this, better than the foolish
tantrums of my heart.

i clutch the gore of summer in my hands, the rot of youth between
my teeth.
i have no city i can leave behind.
i have no room where this desire can be a tenant; so, it lives in me
and unfurls in my stomach like a child i will never have.
(the word hippocampus comes from the greek word for a seahorse.
what i mean is: i am a single parent to this longing.)

to me, you are the sum of my desire, destiny, destination.
i want you, because wanting you is the easiest thing i have ever done.
i want you beyond audacity, beyond the indignity of desire.

i want you. is desire good?

(in my dreams, i trace the feverfew moles on the nape of your
neck. nobody is in a hurry to wake up. the morning is fresh linen, it
rains soda pop outside; all our windows, blurred, a fizz. the bed is
our enterprise of love. we stay in because we want to.

we stay in because nobody needs to exit the hippocampus.)

AN ESCAPE ROOM CALLED SUMMER

the polymer chain of daylight,

the elastic temperate day,

my tropics of summer,

and the plasticity of memory.

That **SUMMER, THE CARNIVAL**
Befell upon us
Onley street rigged out
With bouncing castles and magic tricks
The wooden horses, the rabbit caps
And you, blue pea
Cut in two.

Every evening, you entered a coffin
You swayed your entire body at the crowd
And said, *closer, baby look.*
You were used
To being sawed in half, cauterized
spread open *just like that*
But you always came
right back up
Whole meal whole.

Your horse hoof sly grin
My carousel chest,
Fucking in tents, and of course, the brief goodbye
The imminent *poof.*

MY MEMORY OF SUMMER,
THE MEMORY OF YOU.

I am inside a train
crossing Ely
in hopes of crossing over to you.

I am inside a train
and the seat beside me is empty.

Ely is a cathedral city –
erstwhile isle of the Fens
where the great river Ouse runs
and runners run
the Ely eel course.

We spend the summer
in a city named after a fish.
You, your cat, and her eponym –
Hennessey, Henny, Hen.
I spend my summer with a feline with feathers
her fur, the softest
between us two.

Loose tongued, tipsy lipped
We played house by Chapelfields.
Feta, walnut, cream cheese
Sunbathed, ate aubergine
Fava, flatbread, Turkish tea.
This summer, my flesh
CRÈME BRÛLÉE
Between your teeth.
I named all our linen tricks.

Chill the custard. Place it in a hot bath.

The Bitter Fuck: Cold brew, sweet vanilla cream. The coffee on tap, my mind on you and your lazy fucking smile against Victoria when the sun sinks down and clenches our Ganges breaking over this city. Coffee is a tough ask; I wish we never touched. I will be flying out to Zurich, do you wanna do this on a weekend before our timezones lapse? I almost trade the bitter, for your whiskey breath in my morning routines.

Whisk the warm cream into the yolks.

The I-Am-Tough-As-A-Tusk Fuck: To eviscerate my longing, you have to poach the desire out of my hands and prune it to fit around your horizontals. Our mouths are not language, like love isn't compatibility. Like speed which is only time. Like us. Born with our fists clenched and spending the rest of it white-knuckling.

Bake until set.

The Nostalgic Fuck: I had a nice time, thank you - what did you say your name was? The mole on your thigh reminds me – was it you that liked getting choked? Sometimes, we fuck to live in the past; when we want this city in a snow globe, and our argument about haggis the only thing in memory. A litany of impulsive unbuttoning because I liked your *u up* a lifetime ago and because the button between us has ceased to exist.

Torch the top to caramelize.

The Revenge Fuck: A civil war. Do your worst. I am here because I don't want to be here. "You can fuck the fucking out of your system but not the void." I love you-ing each other after one-night stands. Coping mechanisms, distractions, mercury retrograde, escapism. It's self- destruction on Zoloft. I need a new prescription.

Gently tap the brittle top of melted sugar.

The We-Were-Over-Before-We-Began Fuck: I don't love you; I just want you without an agenda. Do the whole gig – hold hands during a Xavier Dolan, nitro press, book hunt, Agnes Martin, *Zarathustra*. Fuss over your fevered head, kiss you without motives. Learn to love a river for you. Learn to love a fish. Learn to love the way love happens to other people, the way hunger can be stretched thin.

The brittle top of melted sugar that cracks
The brittle top of melted sugar
The brittle top

C

R

A

C

K

S

i write to you from norwich,

a city which gives me bedsores./a city obfuscating/the rigel over poplars perpendicular to my spite./on my back i look up/and there is **THE HUNTER'S DOG** licking lips with weeping willows./often in desire i have been both. in denial i am/the sword taut/unreleased unrepenting/seared over/yews hulking in a jaffa cake sky./devout loneliness curls my tongue and amputates my chest./the teal turns tangerine/*firozi*/i hope/it carries this blue across/river yare/the blue/which says: tear me here./tearing open/the norfolk sky/so deep in its dye, i think it must be the skin of a planet,/the rind of a universe./a possibility/that stamps/might percolate into first snow over your grief river./when i write to you, i write/to turn words into loose change for the ferryman

for styx when we get there

16

at the riverside retail park

inside poundland

under the swinging banner of aisle three

we could share

a hotdog in the april dusk

outside the sun, a prick of blood

swimming in a purple sky–

the colour of your knuckles clenched

during a fasting cbc

your fist clutching

my ketchup'ed pinky

the refrigerator staring back at us,

baring open its cured meat smile

our everyday

squabbling   haggling

butchering   budgeting

in retail aisles. a lick of mustard

at your mouth's end. i want to french you like

alain delon in *plein soleil*. **WE COULD COOK**

MEATBALLS FOR DINNER, we could leave

the delhi metro behind–

we could do taxes on an excel sheet

make 2-for-1 grocery lists

ration our rice.

we could drink a hellish drip

at some hellish café. sunday mornings.

toothpaste kiss.

do you think we could have had that life?

KAASH[1]

cromer ebbs into may/from the right/side of sorrow./the sea scaffolds the sky./willowing the wind wistful, the year/ chases spring for three months/before it arrives. this year it arrives/with shells shrapnel storm clouds flashing fish scales/ conifer cones boughing branches bright./as if, tangerines/by the dozen./my friend says, this is confirmation/bias./we see what we want/to see. copper coin moon,/bunny on its flattop, lunar/pareidolia./hear what we want/to hear. birdsong/equals civilization./our third anniversary plagued./a springstorm./ troubleshooting in maa's kitchen garden where parrots eat/ sun seeds./she fixes the soil with her tuning fork fingers. i lie/ under norfolk/poplars and keep comparing odysseus to behula,[2] both husks on water./mouth of the moon/does my face flash/ against your copper fishchime?/my *nostos* a ripple effect/on wild sugarcanes – milk and seafroth./with a foxtail in my hand, i chase you/your lunar landscape, your marble forest/of কাশ[3] –

---

1   *Kaash* – "I wish" in Urdu.

2   Behula carried the corpse of her husband on a raft, jour-neyed to heaven to bring him back. Homer's hero, stalling in seas, sailing towards Penelope who birthed Pan in Ithaca.

3   Saccharum spontaneum is a grass native to the Indian Subcontinent. It resembles foxtail. It is white in colour.

WHITE

wild garlic, bluebells sticking skeletal
ribs against the norfolk sky where the sun is a clinical, phenyl white

hey sun, what happens when stars die?
like all living things, gravity takes over.

the star eats itself. eats the body. eats the helium core, eats the fuel self.
the light reaches and reaches and reaches. touches you, touches me.
       does not
go out because energy can never be destroyed, only repurposed.

between us. what does happen when stars die?
they die slow, born once, burn slow.
blackhole supernova a nebula then an annihilation.
lightyears take eons take centuries take years; time is light. time is white
when returned faithfully.

light has no colour,
has all. insistence.

there is no agency in being a metaphor. i think it must be miserable
being water, only reflecting what's been given, scattering what's closest,
what can be scattered, calling it blue. the only way water turns
white
when waves crash
we see no colour
we see distance
between each particle measured in light

(between us we have lightyears and a landmass, a language, a body
brined)

when waves crash water
                falls
                    as a fact

like all living things, gravity takes over.
like all living things.
like all living.

<u>6AM</u>

At dawn when mist descends on Norwich
the market breaks its first enchilada sale
the smell of fire and meat sinks
into hollow stomachs
through hollow throats.

The sun haloes the warblers
their fledglings rush rip tear through the wind
like children chasing scabs bloody in sandpits
their quick, small-bellied motion speed-bumping the air
warbling recess laughter from wings.

<u>9AM</u>

My melancholy meets E. Munch for breakfast.
I touch the world with my teeth.
I eat the **GOLDEN SYRUP SOLSTICE**
and read *Revelations* of Julian.
I feel summer simmer
in ceramic teacups.
The long shadow of the sun falls
oblique on yew trees.

<u>12PM</u>

I am beneath our sycamore once again.
Chlorophyll
leaves
the tree
blanched, colourless
glittering

speckled
snow
polka
white
in the dense of the blue forest.

Raven shadows, reddened barks.
The gingko stretching its branch towards the sky
in devotion; the way a pine holds its seeds –
paperweights trapping breeze. Boughs, broken bokeh by the sun.

3PM
The lull of the afternoon
domestic lilacs drooping
along the slow
soft curves of Yare

the thud of magnolia falling
full bodied
flower corpse on forest floors.

6PM
Two deer steadfast
in front of the Sainsbury Centre
their snouts swift and nimble
their hooves on the grass
making the rabbits tremble, their burrowing frantic.

9PM

I am under the trees once again.

I watch the sun wane behind windows.

The Norfolk night

dotting, doting

the Wensum

dark

demure

daystruck.

12AM

At midnight, the noise

that my heart makes

(bihaag)[4]

the parting,

(biyog) –[5]

the distance between my tongue and your teeth

this distance, the empty space

the earth and its axis

the distance between my island-of-one and yours.

---

4   Bihaag is an Indian classical *raga* sung at midnight

5   Biyog – Minus, or separation.

You are hot sake in **MISATO**,
as it rains unceremoniously once again,
and London grovels
at my feet
for a bit of warm rice.

I am a soothsayer, with a five-year plan
to foster a lonely loft in SoHo.

In the mirror,
you are baby faced Godard;
21 and a partygoer
in Eric Rohmer's *Sign of Leo*.

At arm's length,
you flash your Hugh Grant grin
your tectonic tongue; a misfired gun
an ostiary, the mouth of a river,
a trip wire on most Saturdays
when you talk about Baudelaire,
or Knopfler –
all casual braggadocio.

And, I want my violent knuckles
to knot your grapevine hair.
I want to reset my fate,
because you think the fate of a poet
can only be an anecdote for hunger.

You say, you are not responsible
for your thumb, a casual pedestrian
around my piccadilly navel.
"*Yeh pyaar ka izhaar nahi –* "

This is not a love song.

You want to be in big cities,
drunk on branding and optimization
searching for homegrown *amaltas*
on an empty stomach
only to leave
with your mouth brimming
with sunbeams, in quest
for silences amidst the din of takeout warfare.

And, I have been looking at words which move silently.
And, it is not your fault if you were never moved by the silence.

You want to be seen on the big screen,
behind the sheen and veneer of language
occupying space, imagination, algorithms.

You want to be in big cities
For clean air and running tracks;
And I, to make a living.

SUMMER DEPARTING AT GATE 27, TERMINAL 2, HEATHROW

Welcome back to Vodafone, India. Thank you for roaming with Vi!

The plane touches Kandahar
before it touches the rugged topography
of the Hindu Kush, the vast glacial white yeti-bodied mountains.
Despite the enduring geopolitical conflicts; the Kandahar variety
of pomegranate is a favourite at home.
"Do you want me to pack tiffin for you before you go?" Maybe the
            pickled fish
could be one more reason for them to hold me back at border
            control, Maa.

Just give me the pomegranates.

You rain the red
little stones on hung curd
they perforate the surface, they cluster.
Melanocytes. *Alta*[6]
on your hand, Maa. The red,
festive, beautiful. Vermillion without any occasion.
I feel the seeds in my one small stomach
like ground mica in the sky – glittering, grainy, angry little dots.
Your fist full of *anar,*[7]
Maa
hilted rubies inside
MY HANDSOME MOUTH,
that confuses বেদানা[8] with বেদনা[9] —

---

6   Red Dye used to decorate the hands and feet of brides and
married Hindu women.

7   Pomegranate.

8   Pomegranate. Pronounced *be-da-na.*

9   Grief. Pronounced *be-do-na.*

Grief is the hardest thing to carry in a body, Maa.

I eat mine as second helping.

Grief is so dense, Maa. My lungs fight my mouthful.

I knife grief like a birthday cake.

I swallow grief, I swallow it whole.

I ration my sadness to stomach it better.

A deer and a cow have eight stomachs between them.

An earthworm has five hearts. An octopus has three.

This division of labour might make it hurt less, maa.

An assembly line of valves dividing the pain into equal parts.

I can't wash this stain off, Maa; there is no laundry cycle for grief.

So, please cut the fruit for me, mother.

The halved orb, the carmine damp.

IN THE KITCHEN, I HUNGER

for your tungsten mouth.

sodium filament
35mm film roll
simmered in vinegar,
your tongue,
a streak
of lightleak licking
the knife: a salad apple slice.

you eggshell me –
my hard cracks.
roll me white
freeze me, tender.

i wash *masoor*[10] in the sink
the packet says: "all pulses require soaking"
my heart stammers
a pressure cooker whistle
ringing in my ears. i run
my wrists under water,
"all pulses require soaking" –

you bloom forsythias on my arm.
in this darkroom dinner table,
you have me eating out of your palms.

─────────────
10   Red lentils.

Painter at the easel, drained
Oil paint, turpentined.
Biography burdened. Optics,
light tricks, colour wheels. Communication:
this is how I see the world. Dual eyed: green sad and blue sad.
Raingreen against a slatesky.

In the shack there was a shag a *sutta* impasto. There was courage
          behind the cuts,
The bravery bandaged. A drip period followed. Alkali liquid
Paint. Plumes. Pointillism.
Painter at the easel. Quarantined. Cannot draw
A lover's eyes. The corpse eyes, the dead eyes, the closed eyes.
(I just can't get the hands right.)

Hello little magpie, I heard you mate for life.
I thought you were wind chimes, *pica* – mimesis.
There are no songbirds in skyscrapers. Simulacra cement nests.
No space for two.

Come *pica*, be my neighbour.
There is shakshuka, tempera, and *bhurji*[11]
to be made.
You can omnivore my canteen empty.
EVEN PAINTERS HAVE APPETITES.

---

11   Scrambled eggs.

আনারস[12]

after Wong Kar-wai & Leslie Chung

we are packed like sardines on the plane.

fate, faye thought, brought her not to california
palms but into rickety air pocket aisles which
smelled of piss and pineapple chicken.

we sit in front of the loo all day; tumbleweed.

at our closest point we are just 0.01 cm apart from
each other. may finds it funny that our names rhyme.

she is why i hate summers.

she assorts fruit cups and i, juice packets. their
longevity, up in the air. we chop stale stiff bread for
the passengers. i dream of the golden gate.

my tunnel vision. her fisheye way of looking.

she wonders why i fold paper-napkins into plane
tickets.

she peels me

mandarins

---

12   Pineapple

the air is thick with zest. i wonder what it's like to fuck in our tight little city. may laughs, tells me,

she will sink me in bath salts to cool my skin. we both live in the mandarin built in 1963. i ask her if she genuinely salts *all* her canned fruits, she tells me to dice the sunny flesh, warning me to learn why we should not clean up after those who live in muddled memory.

but what about daffy?

dearest daffy, on the fin of the plane pouring salt on his wounds because memory has no shelf-life.

(beloved daffy,

at our closest point we were usually just 0.01 cm apart from each other. there was just 0.01cm between

my flesh and the soft landing.)

I PRACTICE
EMPTY BOTTLES WITH YOU.

You kiss my wrist, and the henna rises to my cheeks.
The lawsone molecules oxidise overnight. Our evening's dredge at
       the bottom.
The waxing gibbous moon peering perilously into the Future, and
       the many ponds of this town.

Tell me was my neck set in the motion of a no?
My night-haul overwrought with vehement ways of exit cues.
I know my throat is good for it.
So, tell me, did I risk a taste of it?
Our fossil limbs entangled somewhere in the *Bherikhana* Lane,
       my unwilling eyes on you and the
way you cup your lips around the embers of tobacco.

Tell me, did I escape this one too?
This cramped town and its nefarious attempts at being called home.

like the dense crowns titlting... like trees so incredibly shy of touching each other,

our small heads.

When it rains abysmally in December,
My neighbourhood floods Calcutta
with second-hand Shakespeare.
Words get replaced by water in our bodies.
(Does loneliness?)
Streetcars don't chime like Christmas charms at 2PM,
And there are potholes everywhere at *boi para* –

In this part of the city,
Western White symbols for progress arrived later.
First, there was the double political murder at the *chowrasta*
cementing all sorts of political vendetta in the Party *istehaar.*
And, of course, the ever-present unsolicited hands on my
          unformed body.

This is what ties a house together – knowing your place and
knowing nothing beyond anger.

I count on my knuckles the number of white wisps in my mother's
          hair,
And she shows me her knuckles turning white at her own
          mother's temper.
So, when it rains, I remember, why I keep fisting at one-way ticket
          departures.

Travel-sore and charred, I sit. I bleed.
A brass goddess, hidden beneath flowers –
"Evermore spring of benediction, bless us fertile."
The women ululate, piercing the darkness like cicadas.

A big palm *pankha* swivels, like elephant ears fending her
        newborn from flies.
Idolatry in isolation; I am banished from the house as long as I bleed.
My fertility tucked between my legs.

This is what ties a family together – **RITUALS,**
telling you who is permitted inside and who never will be.

we were a family of farmers.
we ate salt with our water.
then the river ate our land.
water recurs eternally.
it fits how it falls.
and it falls too easy.

when the water recedes, we clean
the fungible rot with kerosene.

the monsoon has memory.

the rain remembers us, tiger-crouched
our eyes like forest cleanings.

the storm enters our house.
she rips my rind.
there are deserted rooms
in my chest, she fills it
with analogue fire.

on the other side of the river, i
enter to exit.
i douse i,
i, ward of the blues.

blue is the hottest
where blue burns the most.

---

13   Shifting (slash-and-burn) agriculture practiced in parts of
India and Bangladesh is called jhoom.

Jupiter outside my window,

You remind me of everything I want forgotten: the jacaranda years of my violent youth, it's deep lilac shadow in my chest curled up like a dog in the winter sun.

I am coming back to the city. I have vacuum sealed all my belongings. My postcards, and Turner skies, my Vasant Kunj spice-box, my Norfolk loneliness, and all my mid-transit paperbacks. There is a tiny window between my destinations, a slit of a layover in Delhi, and in the haze of jet lag, I can pretend the Qutub Minar is the Shard - or worse, Howrah, the Tower Bridge. The thing about skylines is that if you have looked at them enough to eventually look beyond and then through, it is all urban ennui all city sadness all steel.

I have come too far, too far. I have outgrown my childhood bedroom – I am a giant in a cardboard box, my limbs getting scraped in the process. With my arms jutting out, I am a dryad in the Himalayas as I walk cliff to cliff. My feet now are claws, my beloved mountain, I cannot touch you without hurting you; my hands so cruel in their grip.

I didn't know you could measure the height of a cosmic cliff in light years – is the distance between two points really so far that it needs light to exist? I think that's a cruel way of saying: *how long till you get here*?

And, 'long' is both distance and duration.
And, time is how much we are willing to travel.

The Car: a synonym
to this moment slackened
in backseats
our knees two magnets
held inaccurately.
The tension forcing us to pull away & pull apart
riptide
gravity
conjoined at the mercy of a steering wheel.
If the car leans right, we might crash into the synonym for this
          moment: Desire.
Dearly beloved —
I fear the word which might replace it.

The Accelerator: the tongue
is a transgression and a transgressor
if you're not careful. My tongue crawls
around in circles, the center of its sin – you.
I kissed you and hoped it would be an act
of forgiveness. Tell me which alphabet annihilates
this distance between my organ and yours.
Tell me I am wrong and there is no such thing
as sin in our consignment
of faith. Dearly beloved —
you are yet to make a devout out of me.

The Fog-Light: my August breath,
hair in your hands, an unwelcome homecoming.
The city pellucid
in monsoon. My tongue, the trees,

Dearly beloved, I want to put my roots in you – let me.

The Rear-View: your eyes
ate me before
your mouth did. Dearly beloved —
the synonym for this, is hunger.

The Sun-Roof: awning, my speech garbled
the city wind incoming. **EXEMPT
ZONES** for language. My heart
during take-off. Dearly beloved —

I want to cross borders for you.

THE BODY IS LANGUAGE. it says
come back to the cave with me.
we will whet our nails against the granite wall.

make fire of our bones.

eyes closed, we will shadowfond each other.
we will lie with the roots.

> outside
> telephone wires
> outside
> the traffic
> towers
>
> over us
> ensnares us in talk.

when plato talks about the cave, i think
he means the womb.

THE ÉMIGRÉ.

Let's mop up
the ruins of the Empire
with a bit of a butter naan.

~~GET BEHIND ME MY TONGUE, THIS IS NO LAND FOR YOU~~
~~TO REST~~
~~TO BE FALSE JUDGEMENT IN A DOG'S MOUTH.~~
~~I CAN'T EXACTLY BE HOMESICK IF I LIVE UNDER~~
~~FASCISTS EVERYWHERE.~~

ACKNOWLEDGEMENTS

The *heir of sisyphus* was written mostly in Norwich while I was studying for my M.A. in Creative Writing at the University of East Anglia. My greatest thanks thus, must go to my classmates and professors, and to that collective spirit of collaboration and mentorship which I was lucky to have accrued in our many poetry workshops.

To the friends I made in Norwich, our shared moments of inspiration have inevitably woven themselves into my words. Thank you for the long walks, the much day drinking, the occasional cookouts, and the spurious visits to London, Cambridge, and the beach.

My sincerest gratitude to Aaron Kent at Broken Sleep Books, for having generously invested his time, expertise, and insight into shaping this pamphlet. Thank you for the excellent cover, and as always, for bringing the best out in my poetry.

To *Gutter Magazine* & *bath magg* for providing initial platforms to three of the poems in this pamphlet, and to the larger literary community for their support and encouragement.

To my friends across +91/+44 or whichever timezones we find ourselves in – your camaraderie has always shaped not only my art but also my character. Thank you for loving me into a better writer.

And, finally to Maa & Babai, for guiding me ever upward. I love you. Thank you for the Unconditional.

And to you, of course. Dear reader, for finding me at the right place, at the right time. Thank you.

LAY OUT YOUR UNREST

www.ingramcontent.com/pod-product-compliance
Lightning Source LLC
LaVergne TN
LVHW041238080426
835508LV00011B/1265